Koko's Story

by Dr. Francine Patterson

photographs by Dr. Ronald H. Cohn

SCHOLASTIC INC.

New York   Toronto   London   Auckland   Sydney

For Koko and Michael.

Acknowledgments

*We would like to thank
Martha Pichey, Barbara Hiller,
Jean Feiwel, and Grace Maccarone
for their invaluable help
in the preparation of this book.*

ISBN 0-590-41364-3

Copyright © 1987 by The Gorilla Foundation.
Photographs copyright © Ronald Cohn/The Gorilla Foundation/
National Geographic Society.
Art Direction by Diana Hrisinko. Text design by Emmeline Hsi.
All rights reserved. Published by Scholastic Inc.

12 11 10 9 8 7 6 5 4 3   1 2 3/9
Printed in the U.S.A.   34

"Fine animal gorilla."

—Koko

preface

THE IDEA OF communicating with animals has captured our imaginations from the earliest times. If we could communicate with them, what would animals tell us about themselves and their world? As a graduate student at Stanford University, I became fascinated with this question.

Could I teach a gorilla to communicate with me? I didn't know, but I wanted to try. Other scientists had taught chimpanzees to communicate with humans, but no one had tried this with a gorilla. I would be the first.

I began my work with Koko the same way others had begun a project with a chimp — by trying to teach Koko American Sign Language, or ASL for short. This is a sign language used by more than three hundred thousand deaf Americans. ASL is not "finger spelling" of the alphabet. It would take too long to communicate that way. Instead, ASL takes shortcuts. Movements made with the face, hands, arms, and body can all be signs for complete words or ideas. When you read what Koko has signed, you will notice how sign language leaves out many unnecessary words.

Koko has made more progress in her use of language than I ever thought possible. She uses sign language to rhyme, to joke, and even to tell lies. My life with Koko is full of surprises, and sometimes frustration, for even though Koko is very lovable, she can be a stubborn gorilla. I will never stop teaching Koko and, in her own way, I'm sure she will never stop teaching me. This is the story of what life has been like for both of us since Project Koko began in 1972.

Koko signing "go."

Young Koko

KOKO was born at the San Francisco Zoo on the fourth of July in 1971. She was named Hanabi-Ko, a Japanese word meaning "fireworks child," but everyone called her Koko.

She was three months old when I first saw her, a tiny gorilla clinging to her mother's back. I asked the zoo director if I could try to teach her sign language. He said no.

I didn't get my chance to work with her until one year later. Soon after I had first seen Koko, she became very sick. A terrible illness had spread through the gorilla colony. Koko almost died, but was nursed back to health by doctors and staff at the zoo. Her mother had been unable to care for her, and now Koko lived at the Children's Zoo. She was healthy again, but could not yet live among older gorillas.

I started visiting Koko at the zoo every day. At first, I didn't think Koko liked me. She ignored me. She bit me when I tried to pick her up. Slowly, though, because I never failed to come see her every day, Koko began to trust me.

Each morning, I would carry her around the zoo on my back to visit the other animals. When we passed the baby elephant, Koko would cling to me tightly, scared by the loud trumpeting noise the elephant made whenever we went near.

I first attempted to teach Koko just three words in sign language: *drink, food,* and *more.* I taught the zoo assistants who helped in the nursery to form the sign "food" with their hands. They used this sign whenever they gave Koko anything to eat.

"Drink," I signed each time I gave Koko her bottle.

I formed her small hand into the sign for "drink," too.

One morning, about a month after I began working with Koko, I was slicing fruit for her snack. Koko was watching me.

"Food," she signed.

I couldn't believe my eyes.

"Food," she clearly signed again. Koko had communicated with me! I wanted to jump for joy. Koko could sense I was happy with her. She became so excited that she grabbed a bucket, plunked it over her head, and ran wildly around the playroom.

Koko signing "lipstick."

Koko sliding headfirst down the slide at the San Francisco Zoo.

By age two, Koko's signs were more than just simple, one-word requests like "up," "drink," and "more." Now Koko was learning signs quickly and stringing them together.

"There mouth, mouth-you there," Koko signed when she wanted me to blow fog on the nursery window to draw in with our fingers.

"Pour that hurry drink hurry," she signed when she was thirsty.

Koko had a big birthday party when she turned three. One of her presents was a pair of toy binoculars.

"Look," she signed, marching proudly with the binoculars around her neck.

She carefully ate almost all of her birthday cake with a spoon. But when it came time for the last bite, Koko couldn't resist. She scooped the cake up with her hand and stuffed it into her mouth.

"More eat," she signed.

On her birthday, we forgave her for such table manners.

Koko Leaves the Zoo

KOKO was three when we decided to move to the grounds of Stanford University, where I was a graduate student. Here she would be able to meet with a young male gorilla from a nearby wildlife park. It was much quieter here than at the Children's Zoo. I hoped our new location would help Koko concentrate on her language lessons without any distractions.

At first, Koko was like any frightened gorilla. She made angry display charges at the door of her trailer.

"Go home," she signed, wanting to get out. She didn't know yet that this new site for her trailer *was* home. Sometimes she had nightmares and cried in her sleep. I stayed with her in the trailer every night until she was used to her new home, and she no longer made the low "whoo-whoo" sound of a gorilla crying.

Once she had settled into her new home, Koko began to make great progress. She started using language in surprising ways. She would listen to me ask her a question in English, and she would respond in sign. One day she overheard me saying the word *candy,* a word she learned to refer to her chewable vitamins.

"Candy, candy, do have candy," Koko signed, hoping she was in for a special treat.

I learned my lesson. When speaking to someone else, I would spell words like candy if Koko was nearby.

By the age of five Koko knew more than 200 words in sign. I recorded every sign that Koko used, and even videotaped her actions so I could study her use of sign language later. The more signs Koko learned, the more she showed us her personality. She argued with me, displayed a very definite sense of humor, and expressed strong opinions.

"You have pretty eyes," a visitor signed to Koko upon meeting her.

Koko stroked her finger across her nose.

"False," was the sign Koko chose for her answer.

Koko even used sign language to tell lies. Once I caught her poking the window screen of her trailer with a chopstick.

"What are you doing?" I signed to her.

Koko quickly put the stick in her mouth.

"Mouth smoke," she answered, pretending to be "smoking" the chopstick. One time I caught her chewing a crayon when she was supposed to be drawing a picture.

"You're not eating that, are you?" I asked Koko.

"Lip," Koko signed. She quickly took the crayon out of her mouth and moved it across her lips, as if putting on lipstick. She didn't fool me!

Koko used to have a bad habit of breaking plastic spoons. My friend Ron knew how to stop her from doing that.

"Good! Break them," Ron signed.

Koko put down the spoon she was about to bend. I could tell she had another idea. Koko picked up another spoon and started kissing it instead.

When Koko is very bad, she is sent to a corner in her trailer.

"Stubborn devil," she signs to herself. She knows she has been naughty. If it is only for a small thing, she will excuse herself after a little while. But if she has been very bad, she soon turns around to get my attention.

"Sorry," Koko signs. "Need hug."

But Koko was more often playful than naughty, using sign language to let me know when she wanted to play a game.

"Time quiet chase," she signed, when she wanted to play hide-and-seek.

"Koko, where are you?" I'd call out. I'd look in the oven and search through the cupboards. I would always act very surprised when she came out from where she was hiding.

Koko even used the signs she had learned to play jokes on people. One day, my friend Barbara saw Koko building a nest out of white towels.

"That red," Koko was signing to herself.

"You know better, Koko. What color is it?" Barbara asked.

"Red, red, red," Koko kept signing.

Barbara gave up. She had thought Koko had learned the sign for white. But she saw Koko grinning.

"Red," signed Koko again. Then Koko carefully picked a speck of lint off one of the white towels. Koko held it up for Barbara to see. What color was it? Red!

Koko and Michael

W HEN KOKO was five years old, I thought it was time to find a gorilla companion for her. One day I said to Koko, "A new baby is arriving." She was pleased by the idea of a baby.

"Wrong, old," Koko signed to me when she first saw the frisky little gorilla.

This playmate did not fit Koko's idea of a baby. The new gorilla was already more than three years old. He had been named King Kong. I changed his name to Michael, because gorillas do not act like King Kong. They are usually very shy and gentle creatures.

I wanted to teach a second gorilla sign language, and I also hoped that one day Koko and Michael would mate and have a baby gorilla.

We started to teach Michael sign language as soon as he came to live with us. Of course, he hasn't learned as many signs as Koko yet, but Michael is a good student. He often concentrates even longer on his lessons than Koko does.

At first, Koko was very jealous of her new playmate. She called Michael names, and blamed him for things he hadn't done.

"Stupid toilet," Koko signed, when asked about Michael.

"Stink bad squash gorilla," Michael answered back.

Koko loved to see Michael get scolded, and sometimes it was for doing something that Koko encouraged him to do. She would listen to me telling Michael to be a good gorilla.

"Huh, huh, huh, huh," was the sound Koko made. She was making the deep, breathy sound of a gorilla laughing.

Koko signing "eat."

But Koko and Michael also loved to play together, and signed to each other often.

"Tickle, please," signed Koko, tapping her armpit. Michael would jump toward her to find a good spot to tickle. Then they would wrestle together. They banged on the walls, tumbled, and kicked. It was rough, but it was still play.

Koko signing "tickle."

Koko and Michael loved to ride in my car at Stanford.

"Go there," Koko would sign, acting like a backseat driver. She knew exactly where the soda machines were located at the university, and would point the way. On special occasions, she would climb out of the car and put a quarter in the soda machine. Some students were very surprised to see Koko grab a can of soda and climb back into my car!

"Turn turn," she would then sign, pointing to the right and to the left. She did that just to make the ride longer, especially when she knew we were getting close to home.

Koko's Pets

BEFORE KOKO had her first kitten named All Ball,
she played with many small animals. Koko once
befriended a blue jay. The baby bird had lost its mother,
so I kept it in a cage and fed it many times each day.
I took the caged bird to Koko's room.

"Open that," Koko signed, pointing to the
cage door.

I opened the door and out flew the blue jay.

"Like that. Nice have," she signed.

"Do you have a name for him?" I asked Koko.

"Tongue," Koko answered.

"Yes, he has a tongue," I said. "But what will you
name him?"

"Tongue," she signed again. Maybe Koko chose
that name because she saw the bird's tongue as it
opened its mouth wide, asking for food.

Koko was fascinated by the small tree frogs she saw in her yard near the trailer. These little frogs could change color — from green to red to gold. I wouldn't catch one for Koko at first. I was afraid she might accidentally hurt the small creature. But one day Koko found one in her playground.

"Underarm," she signed, showing me where she gently kept her new friend. Koko carried the tree frog under her arm in a place that is shaped like a pocket. A gorilla can hold things there and move freely. But the tree frog jumped out!

Koko had a special way of catching it. She placed her big furry foot on the tip of the little frog's foot.

She'll squash it! I thought, when I first watched her do that. But Koko never did. She'd catch a small part of its foot and then reach down to pick it up. It was funny to watch such a big gorilla trying to catch a tiny frog.

Koko signing "ball."

Koko had played with other kittens before she had All Ball. But All Ball was the first pet Koko ever had of her very own.

"Koko love Ball. Soft good cat cat," she signed.

Then All Ball was killed by a car just before Christmas in 1984. I had to tell Koko what happened. At first Koko acted as if she didn't hear me. Later, she told us how she felt.

"Cry, sad, frown," Koko signed.

"What happened to All Ball?" I asked her.

"Blind, sleep cat," she answered.

"We don't see him anymore, do we?" I said.

We were both very sad.

"What do you want for Christmas this year?" Koko's friend Barbara asked her a few days later.

"Want cat," Koko signed.

"Like that," she signed, pointing to a picture of a cat without a tail. But when a furry orange kitten came to stay with Koko, it kept running away from her.

"Do you have a name for your kitty?" I asked her.

"Lips, lipstick," Koko signed.

Koko signing "alligator."

Michael also had a name for Koko's new kitten. "Banana. My cat red," Michael signed. He had been watching Koko and her new kitten. He wanted a pet, too.

So Koko's second kitten was given to Michael. Koko finally chose another, a soft gray one.

"Baby. Visit gorilla," she signed.

"Have you thought of a name yet?" I asked her.

"That smoke. Smoke smoke," she answered.

The kitten was a smoky gray, so we named her Smoky.

When Koko is asked what her favorite animal is, she always signs, "gorilla." But Koko does not like *all* animals. She is afraid of the same animal that gorillas in the wild fear: the crocodile. I used to hang rubber alligators above objects she wasn't allowed to touch. They looked a lot like crocodiles to Koko. But now that she is older these rubber alligators don't scare her so much. She can even hold one to play her favorite practical joke. She sneaks up on a friend with the toy alligator behind her back. Then she whips it out, waving it madly. You are expected to scream and act as terrified as Koko would be if someone played this trick on her.

Koko's Day

WHEN KOKO was eight and Michael was six, we moved again. Now we live in a forested area in Woodside, California, where there is more room for both gorillas to play outside. Koko and Michael still live in a big trailer, but they now have their own bedrooms and kitchens.

Koko wakes up by eight-thirty every morning. Breakfast is usually cereal with milk and fruit. On most days she has sign language lessons from nine to ten with her teacher. Koko now knows more than five hundred signs. Two signs that she is learning now are "forget" and "what-for." She also knows signs that stand for airplane, belly button, boring, and surprise. She recently invented two signs — for a pocket and a hearing aid. And by now she knows what C-A-N-D-Y means. Even if I use pig latin, and say, "andy-cay," she knows exactly what I mean!

Penny signing "who?"; Koko signing her name.

By ten o'clock, Koko is tired of her lessons and needs a break.

"Have Mike in," Koko signs to her teacher.

So Koko and Michael play together for about an hour. They might play with Koko's toys, but Koko is still jealous of Michael and isn't always very good about sharing her things. She has a tricycle, dolls, storybooks, rubber dinosaurs, and a skateboard.

"Do you want to ride the skateboard?" I ask Koko.

She frowns at me, but sits down on the board and scoots around the trailer — very slowly. She won't stand on her skateboard alone. Koko has seen me fall too many times.

At eleven, it's time to go back to work. Koko has reading lessons on many mornings. She sees the written word for *cat* and then forms the sign for that word. We can't show her too many pictures of cats, though. She still gets sad when she sees any cat that looks at all like All Ball, her first kitten.

Koko and Michael also take tests. They make mistakes, but some mistakes don't seem like wrong answers to a gorilla. One test question asked Koko to point to two things that are good to eat. Koko saw pictures of a block, an apple, a flower, a shoe, and an ice-cream sundae. Koko pointed to the apple — and the flower, of course.

Sometimes Koko thinks she is being funny when she makes mistakes.

"Nose," she signs, pointing to a picture of a bird's eye.

Then she grabs a toy key and places it on her head.

"Hat," signs Koko. Then she laughs and laughs. She marches around the playroom, waving her hands and grinning. She can't stop chuckling over her own joke. Koko can be a very silly gorilla.

But Koko can also be very stubborn when she is tired of being quizzed. She will stare hard at the right answer but point to the wrong one. Or she will fold her arms and absolutely refuse to continue, staring down at her belly button.

    At noon, Koko has lunch—juice, fresh vegetables,
and soybean cake or another protein.
    "Can you say a long sentence about lunch?" I
ask her.
    "Love lunch eat taste it meat," Koko answers.
    Later in the afternoon, she has a snack. Both Koko
and Michael like peanut butter and fruit sandwiches.
    "Need candy bean," Koko then signs, asking for
her chewable vitamin.

One afternoon, a scientist who studies wild chimpanzees came to see Koko.

"Do you like people to stand up or sit down when they are with you?" I asked Koko.

"Down!" she signed, lying on the floor to prove her point when I repeated the question.

Koko likes quiet friends and is especially gentle with babies and older people.

When Koko meets people for the first time, she gives them the "blow test" by blowing into their faces. Then she uses the signs she knows to find out more about them.

"Fake-tooth?" she signs to see if they have any gold teeth or silver fillings.

Koko also comments on their jewelry and clothes, and may ask to see the contents of a briefcase or purse. She may show off her toys or the posters on her walls.

Koko likes to take photographs and will sometimes hold my friend Ron's camera if he lets her. She loves to watch the flash go off.

"Love camera," she signs.

Dinnertime is around four-thirty, and the meal is almost always fresh vegetables. Koko likes corn on the cob and tomatoes, but she will not eat mushrooms or radishes.

"Dirty stink," she signs, if she sees them on her plate.

Before bed, Koko goes off by herself for "quiet time." Sometimes she looks through a stack of her favorite letters from children. Or Koko might play a scary game with her dolls and dinosaur.

"Teeth, bite," she signs, as she makes the rubber dinosaur attack one of her dolls. The doll squeaks, and Koko quickly picks up the dinosaur and twists it around in the air. Then Koko inspects her doll and starts to kiss it. Then she decides to kiss the dinosaur, and the play acting is over.

Koko likes to look through her picture books, too, or play with Smoky. She brushes Smoky just the way I brush Koko. She keeps her kitten very clean.

At seven o'clock, it's time for Koko and Michael to get ready for bed. I take care of Koko while my friend takes care of Michael. Every night, Koko builds a nest, just as gorillas do in the wild. She makes her "bed" by piling blankets, towels, old clothes, and rugs into a circular nest on top of a flat tire.

"Brush teeth," Koko signs.

I brush her back teeth, but Koko can brush her front teeth by herself. I rub the leathery palms of her hands and feet with baby oil. That way they stay smooth and moist.

Then I give Koko a snack of her favorite foods, such as apples, nuts, and cheese. I call it a "night dish," a treat I hope will make bedtime more fun. Koko always tries to put off going to bed, because she still doesn't like to be left alone at night.

"Tickle there," signs Koko, wanting to tickle me.

"Koko, you know it's time for bed," I tell her.

"That red," she signs, pointing to my shirt. Koko is trying hard to change the subject. But now it's past her bedtime.

"Good-night, Koko," I sign, and tiptoe out of her room. I peek into Michael's room to make sure he is also settled for the night, then walk back to my house just fifty feet away. A small speaker next to my bed lets me listen to any sounds coming from the trailer. Koko and Michael know I am always there if they need me.